The World's Funniest Proverbs

JAMES ALEXANDER

Beauty is in the eye of the beer holder.

Don't take life too seriously – it's not permanent.

Multi-tasking: the art of screwing up everything all at once.

Never marry for money; you will borrow cheaper

Crombie Jardine
PUBLISHING LIMITED

13 Nonsuch Walk, Cheam, Surrey, SM2 7LG
www.crombiejardine.com

This edition was first published by
Crombie Jardine Publishing Limited in 2004
First reprint, 2005

ISBN 1-905102-02-X

Original concept and compilation by Crombie Jardine
Designed by 'Mr Stiffy'
Printed & Bound in Great Britain by
William Clowes Ltd, Beccles, Suffolk

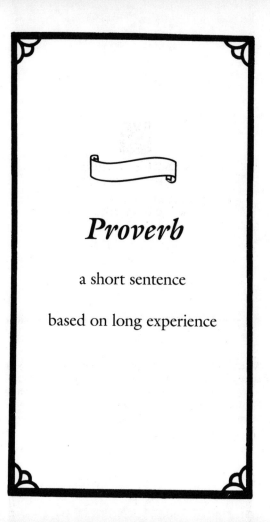

Proverb

a short sentence

based on long experience

CONTENTS

SCHOOL DAYS

A secondary school teacher made a list of some well known proverbs and gave the class the first half of the proverbs, so that they could complete the sayings. Here's what they came up with:

AS YOU MAKE YOUR BED SO
SHALL YOU . . . MESS IT UP.

BETTER TO BE SAFE THAN . . .
HIT A TEACHER.

YOU CAN LEAD A HORSE
TO WATER BUT . . . HOW?

DON'T BITE THE HAND THAT . . .
LOOKS DIRTY.

A MISS IS AS GOOD AS A . . . MR.

YOU CAN'T TEACH AN
OLD DOG . . . MATHS.

THE PEN IS MIGHTIER
THAN THE . . . PIGS.

AN IDLE MIND IS . . .
THE BEST WAY TO RELAX.

THERE'S NO SMOKE
WITHOUT . . . POLLUTION.

A PENNY SAVED . . .
IS NOT MUCH.

TWO'S COMPANY, THREE'S . . .
THE MUSKETEERS.

LAUGH AND THE WORLD LAUGHS WITH
YOU, CRY AND . . . YOU MUST BLOW
YOUR OWN NOSE.

CHILDREN SHOULD BE SEEN
AND NOT . . . SMACKED OR GROUNDED.

WHEN THE BLIND
LEADETH THE
BLIND . . . BEST GET
OUT OF THE WAY.

NEVER UNDERESTIMATE THE
POWER OF . . . TERMITES.

NO NEWS IS . . .
IMPOSSIBLE.

LOVE ALL, TRUST . . . ME.

DON'T PUT OFF TILL TOMORROW
WHAT . . . YOU PUT ON TO GO TO BED.

NONE ARE SO BLIND AS . . .
STEVIE WONDER.

IF AT FIRST YOU DON'T SUCCEED . . .
GET NEW BATTERIES.

PEOPLE IN GLASS
HOUSES SHOULDN'T . . .
RUN AROUND NAKED.

THERE'S NO
FOOL LIKE . . .
UNCLE JOHNNY.

CHINESE PROVERBS

BASEBALL WRONG:
MAN WITH FOUR BALLS
CANNOT WALK.

CROWDED ELEVATOR SMELL
DIFFERENT TO MIDGET.

MAN WHO FART IN CHURCH
SIT IN OWN PEW.

MAN WHO RUN IN FRONT
OF CAR GET TIRED.

MAN WHO RUN BEHIND CAR
GET EXHAUSTED.

MAN WITH HAND IN POCKET
FEEL COCKY ALL DAY.

MAN WHO WALK THROUGH
AIRPORT TURNSTYLE SIDEWAYS
GOING TO BANGKOK.

MAN WHO FIGHT WITH WIFE ALL DAY
GET NO PIECE AT NIGHT.

MAN WHO DRIVE LIKE HELL
BOUND TO GET THERE.

MAN WHO LIVE IN GLASS HOUSE NEED
TO CHANGE CLOTHES IN BASEMENT.

MAN WHO DROP WATCH IN TOILET
BOUND TO HAVE CRAPPY TIME.

MAN WHO WANT PRETTY
NURSE MUST BE PATIENT.

MAN WHO PUSH PIANO DOWN
MINESHAFT GET A FLAT MINER.

PASSIONATE KISS LIKE SPIDER'S WEB:
SOON LEAD TO UNDOING OF FLY.

VIRGINITY LIKE BUBBLE:
ONE PRICK ALL GONE.

LIFE

42% of all statistics
are made up.
(ANON)

Ability is what you are able to do,
motivation determines what
you do, attitude decides how
well you do it.
(ANON)

The absent are always wrong.
(ENGLISH)

Act as if you cannot fail.
(SOUTH AFRICA)

ALL GOOD THINGS COME TO
WHOEVER GETS THERE FIRST.

(ANON)

ALWAYS REMEMBER: YOU'RE UNIQUE.
JUST LIKE EVERYONE ELSE.

(ANON)

AN ANECDOTE IN TIME
SAVES BOREDOM.

(ANON)

A DAY WITHOUT SUNSHINE IS
LIKE . . . NIGHT.

(ANON)

A CLEAN HOUSE IS THE SIGN OF A
MISSPENT LIFE.

(ANON)

A CLEAR CONSCIENCE IS USUALLY THE
SIGN OF A BAD MEMORY.

(ANON)

A MAN SURROUNDED BY PYGMIES
WILL ALWAYS LOOK BIG.

(ANON)

AMBITION WITHOUT KNOWLEDGE IS
LIKE A CANOE WITHOUT A PADDLE.

(ANON)

AN APPLE A DAY KEEPS THE DOCTOR
AWAY. REMEMBER THAT THE NEXT
TIME YOU CAN'T GET AN APPOINTMENT.

(ANON)

ANYTHING WORTH TAKING SERIOUSLY
IS WORTH POKING FUN AT.

(ANON)

AS LONG AS YOUR MISTAKES ARE NEW
ONES YOU CAN ARGUE THAT YOU ARE
MAKING PROGRESS.

(ANON)

BOREDOM IS THE PRICE YOU PAY FOR
STAYING OUT OF TROUBLE.

(ANON)

CRAP OR GET OFF THE POT.

(AMERICAN)

DANGER AND DELIGHT GROW ON THE
SAME STALK.

(ENGLISH)

DISCIPLINE IS MAKING THE CHOICE
BETWEEN WHAT YOU WANT NOW AND
WHAT YOU WANT MOST.

(ANON)

DO NOT FOLLOW THE PATH;
GO WHERE THERE IS NO PATH
AND BEGIN THE TRAIL . . .
(SOUTH AFRICA)

DO NOT INSULT THE MOTHER
ALLIGATOR UNTIL AFTER YOU HAVE
CROSSED THE RIVER.
(HAITIAN)

DON'T BITE THE HAND THAT FEEDS YOU.
THAT'S MASOCHISTIC.
(ANON)

DO NOT WALK BEHIND SOMEONE FOR
THEY MAY NOT LEAD. DO NOT WALK
AHEAD OF THEM, FOR THEY MAY NOT
FOLLOW. DO NOT WALK BESIDE THEM,
EITHER. JUST LEAVE THEM ALONE.
(ANON)

DON'T take Life too
SERIOUSLY;
IT'S NOT PERMANENT.

(ANON)

DON'T WORRY; IT ONLY SEEMS
PERVERTED THE FIRST TIME.
(ANON)

ENSURE YOUR KITCHEN IS KEPT
CLEAN – EAT OUT.
(ANON)

EVERYONE LOVES JUSTICE IN THE
AFFAIRS OF OTHERS.
(ITALIAN)

EXPERIENCE IS SOMETHING YOU GET
JUST AFTER YOU NEED IT.
(ANON)

EXPERIENCE IS A COMB
NATURE GIVES TO MEN
WHEN THEY ARE BALD.
(EASTERN)

EYES TRUST THEMSELVES BUT EARS
TRUST OTHERS.

(GERMAN)

FORTUNE IS BLIND BUT NOT INVISIBLE.

(FRENCH)

GENIUS IS ONE PERCENT INSPIRATION,
NINETY-NINE PERCENT PERSPIRATION.

(THOMAS EDISON)

GOOD JUDGMENT COMES FROM BAD
EXPERIENCE, AND A LOT OF THAT
COMES DIRECTLY FROM
BAD JUDGMENT.

(ANON)

HE WHO SERVES TWO MASTERS HAS
TO LIE TO ONE.
(PORTUGUESE)

HE WHO LAUGHS LAST HASN'T
GOT ALL THE FACTS.
(ANON)

HE WHO SEEKS TROUBLE
NEVER MISSES.
(ENGLISH)

HE WHO SMILES IN A CRISIS HAS FOUND
SOMEONE TO BLAME.
(ANON)

I DON'T KNOW WHAT APATHY IS
AND I DON'T CARE!
(ANON)

If a man does his best,
what else is there?
(General George S. Patton)

If at first you don't succeed,
consider yourself average.

(Anon)

If at first you don't succeed,
parachuting is not the
sport for you.

(Anon)

If we cannot get what
we like, let us like
what we get.

(Spanish)

IF YOU ARE ON A ROAD
TO NOWHERE, FIND
ANOTHER ROAD.
(SOUTH AFRICA)

IF YOU REALLY WANT TO DO
SOMETHING, YOU'LL FIND A WAY; IF YOU
DON'T, YOU'LL FIND AN EXCUSE.

(ANON)

IF YOU WANT TO BE HEARD,
SPEAK UP. IF YOU WANT
TO BE SEEN, STAND UP. IF YOU
WANT TO BE APPRECIATED,
JUST SHUT UP.

(ANON)

INSTINCT IS STRONGER THAN
UPBRINGING.

(IRISH)

IT IS NEVER A GOOD IDEA TO TEST THE
WATER WITH BOTH FEET.

(ANON)

Jealousy and fear
have big eyes.

(Serbian)

Join the army, meet interesting
people, kill them.

(Anon)

Just before dawn is the darkest
hour. So if you're planning to
pinch your neighbour's milk,
that's the time to do it.

(Anon)

Laugh and the whole world laughs
with you, cry and you cry alone.
It's called fair-weathered.

(Anon)

JUST BECAUSE YOU'RE
PARANOID DOESN'T MEAN
THEY AREN'T AFTER YOU.

(ANON)

Life is what happens when you are
making other plans.

(JOHN LENNON)

Listen to your conscience
– the inner voice that tells you
someone might be watching.

(ANON)

Mediocrity has certain
attractions; it's much less
demanding than success.

(ANON)

Never lend your car to anyone to
whom you have given birth.

(ERMA BOMBECK)

NEVER RUB BACKSIDES
WITH A PORCUPINE.
(GHANA)

PERFECT BEHAVIOUR IS BORN OUT OF
COMPLETE INDIFFERENCE.
(OSCAR WILDE)

REALITY IS MERELY A CRUTCH FOR
PEOPLE WHO CAN'T COPE WITH DRUGS.
(ANON)

SECURITY IS AN ILLUSION. LIFE IS
EITHER A DARING ADVENTURE
OR IT IS NOTHING AT ALL.
(HELEN KELLER)

SEX IS LIKE AIR:
IT'S NOT IMPORTANT
UNLESS YOU AREN'T
GETTING ANY.

(ANON)

Sometimes you are the insect;
sometimes you are the
windscreen.

(Anon)

Strategy is better
than strength.

(Nigeria)

Stretch your hands as far as
they reach, and grab all
you can grab.

(Nigeria)

The eyes believe what they see;
the ears what people tell them.

(German)

30

SOMETIMES THE LIGHT
AT THE END OF THE
TUNNEL REALLY IS AN
ONCOMING TRAIN.

(ANON)

SOMETIMES YOU'RE
THE PIGEON,
SOMETIMES YOU'RE
THE STATUE.

(ANON)

THE JOURNEY OF A THOUSAND MILES
STARTS WITH A BROKEN FAN BELT.
(ANON)

THERE'S AN INVERSE RELATIONSHIP
BETWEEN HOW GOOD SOMETHING IS
FOR YOU, AND HOW MUCH FUN IT IS.
(CALVIN AND HOBBES)

THERE IS ONLY ONE PRETTY CHILD
IN THE WORLD, AND EVERY
MOTHER HAS IT.
(CHINESE)

THREE MAY KEEP A SECRET IF
TWO OF THEM ARE DEAD.
(BENJAMIN FRANKLIN)

TOO MANY COOKS SPOIL THE BROTH.
LET SOMEONE ELSE PREPARE DINNER.
(ANON)

TRUE POWER COMES FROM A MIX OF
CO-OPERATION AND SILENCE.
(SOUTH AFRICA)

WHEN THE DOOR IS CLOSED, LEARN TO
SLIDE ACROSS THE CRACK OF THE SILL.
(NIGERIA)

WHEN THE MOUSE LAUGHS AT THE CAT,
THERE IS A HOLE NEARBY.
(NIGERIA)

zZZZ

VIRTUE IS ITS OWN
REWARD. BUT IT'S ALSO
VERY BORING.

(ANON)

WANT A THING LONG ENOUGH
AND YOU DON'T.

(CHINESE)

WELL DONE IS BETTER
THAN WELL SAID.

(BENJAMIN FRANKLIN)

YOU CANNOT SHAKE HANDS
WITH A CLENCHED FIST.

(GANDHI)

YOU HAVE THREE CHOICES IN LIFE: GIVE
UP, GIVE IN, OR GIVE IT YOUR ALL!

(ANON)

PROFESSIONS

A BAD COMPROMISE IS BETTER THAN
a SUCCESSFUL LAW SUIT.

(SPANISH)

A LAWYER'S FEE AND A PROSTITUTE'S
WAGES ARE PAID IN ADVANCE.

(INDIAN)

A LAWYER'S OPINION IS WORTH
NOTHING UNLESS PAID FOR.

(ENGLISH)

A PEASANT BETWEEN TWO LAWYERS
IS LIKE A FISH BETWEEN TWO CATS.

(ANON)

DIPLOMACY IS THE ART OF SAYING
"NICE DOGGIE", WHILST LOOKING
FOR A BIGGER STICK.
(ANON)

DOCTORS CLEAN THE BODY,
MINISTERS THE CONSCIENCE, AND
LAWYERS THE PURSE.
(GERMAN)

HE THAT LOVES THE LAW WILL
GET HIS FILL OF IT.
(SCOTTISH)

A DIPLOMAT IS SOMEONE WHO
CAN TELL YOU TO GO TO
HELL AND HAVE YOU
ACTUALLY LOOKING
FORWARD TO THE TRIP.

(ANON)

It is better to enter the mouth of
a tiger than a court of law.

(CHINESE)

It is better to exist unknown to
the law and lawyers.

(IRISH)

Lawyers and painters can soon
change black to white.

(DANISH)

Lawyers and soldiers are the
devil's playmates.

(GERMAN)

POLITICIANS ARE LIKE
DIAPERS AND NEED TO
BE CHANGED FOR
THE SAME REASON.

(ANON)

NEW LAWS ARE FOLLOWED
BY NEW TRICKS.

(GERMAN)

'VIRTUE IS IN THE MIDDLE,'
SAID THE DEVIL, AS HE SAT DOWN
BETWEEN TWO LAWYERS.

(DANISH)

WHEN GOD WANTED TO PUNISH MAN HE
INVENTED LAWYERS.

(RUSSIAN)

WORK

A DESK WITHOUT PAPERWORK IS A
SIGN OF ONE BORN TO DELEGATE.

(ANON)

A TIDY DESK IS THE SIGN OF A
DISTURBED MIND.

(ANON)

HARD WORK NEVER HURT ANYONE.
BUT THEN WHY RISK IT?

(ANON)

MAKE SURE YOU ARE NOT
IRREPLACEABLE: IF YOU CAN'T BE
REPLACED, YOU CAN'T BE PROMOTED.

(ANON)

MULTI-TASKING: THE ART
OF SCREWING UP
EVERYTHING ALL
AT ONCE.

(ANON)

NOTHING IS SO SIMPLE THAT IT
CANNOT BE SCREWED UP.

(ANON)

OPPORTUNITY IS MISSED BY MOST
PEOPLE BECAUSE IT IS DRESSED IN
OVERALLS AND LOOKS LIKE WORK.

(THOMAS EDISON)

THERE ARE TWO KINDS OF
PEOPLE IN LIFE: PEOPLE WHO LIKE
THEIR JOBS AND PEOPLE WHO DON'T
WORK HERE ANY MORE.

(ANON)

WHEN YOU OWN YOUR OWN
BUSINESS, YOU ONLY HAVE
TO WORK HALF A DAY.
YOU CAN DO ANYTHING YOU
WANT WITH THE OTHER
TWELVE HOURS.

(ANON)

DRINK

A CASK OF WINE WILL WORK
MORE MIRACLES THAN A
CHURCH FULL OF SAINTS.
(ITALIAN)

A DRINK PRECEDES A STORY.
(IRISH)

A DRUNK MAN'S
WORDS ARE A SOBER
MAN'S THOUGHTS.
(ANON)

ALWAYS DO SOBER WHAT YOU SAID
YOU'D DO DRUNK. THAT WILL TEACH
YOU TO KEEP YOUR MOUTH SHUT.
(ERNEST HEMMINGWAY)

BEAUTY IS IN
THE EYE
OF THE
BEER HOLDER.

(ANON)

BEER IS PROOF THAT
GOD LOVES US AND WANTS
US TO BE HAPPY.
(BENJAMIN FRANKLIN)

FOOD WITHOUT WINE
IS LIKE A DAY
WITHOUT SUNSHINE.
(ITALIAN)

GOOD AS DRINK IS,
IT ENDS IN THIRST.
(IRISH)

HE WHO DRINKS ON
CREDIT WILL GET
DRUNK TWICE.
(SERBIAN)

Give a man a fish and
he will eat for a day.
Teach him how to fish,
and he will sit about in
a boat and guzzle
beer all day.

(ANON)

IF ALCOHOL IS A CRUTCH, THEN
WHISKEY IS THE WHEELCHAIR.
(ANON)

IT IS SWEET TO DRINK BUT
BITTER TO PAY FOR.
(IRISH)

ONE DRINK IS ENOUGH, TWO
DRINKS ARE TOO MANY, THREE
DRINKS ARE NOT ENOUGH.
(PORTUGUESE)

THE WINE IS SWEET
BUT THE PAYMENT SOUR.
(IRISH)

THE CHURCH IS CLOSE BUT THE
ROAD IS ICY; THE BAR IS FAR
BUT I'LL WALK CAREFULLY.
(RUSSIAN)

THE DRUNKEN MAN'S
JOY IS USUALLY THE
SOBER MAN'S REGRET.
(DANISH)

THE DRUNKEN MOUTH
LETS SLIP THE
HEART'S SECRETS.
(GERMAN)

THE FIRST DRINK WITH
WATER, THE SECOND
WITHOUT WATER,
THE THIRD LIKE WATER.

(SPANISH)

THERE'S NO HARM
IN THE WINE – IT'S THE
DRUNKENNESS THAT
IS TO BLAME.

(RUSSIAN)

THERE ARE MORE
OLD DRUNKARDS THAN
THERE ARE OLD DOCTORS.
(FRENCH)

WHEN THE DRINK
GOES IN, THE
SECRETS COME OUT.
(ANON)

WHEN THE DRINK
IS INSIDE,
THE SENSE
IS OUTSIDE.
(IRISH)

GETTING OLD

AGE IS A HIGH PRICE TO PAY FOR
MATURITY.

(ANON)

AGE IS JUST MIND OVER MATTER: IF
YOU DON'T MIND, IT DOESN'T MATTER.

(ANON)

A WOLF MIGHT LOSE HIS TEETH BUT
NOT HIS CHARACTER.

(ANON)

BEING YOUNG IS A FAULT THAT
DIMINISHES DAILY.

(SWEDISH)

BE NICE TO YOUR
CHILDREN; THEY'LL BE
CHOOSING THE OLD
FOLKS' HOME.

(ANON)

BY THE TIME YOU ARE OLD
ENOUGH TO APPRECIATE
YOUR PARENTS YOU WILL
HAVE CHILDREN OF YOUR
OWN WHO TAKE YOU
FOR GRANTED.

(ANON)

IF THE YOUNG ONLY KNEW...
IF THE OLD ONLY COULD.
(FRENCH)

INSIDE EVERY OLDER PERSON IS A
YOUNGER PERSON ... WONDERING WHAT
THE HELL HAPPENED.
(CORA HARVEY ARMSTRONG)

THE DIFFERENCE BETWEEN ADULTS
AND CHILDREN IS THAT ADULTS DON'T
ASK QUESTIONS.
(AMERICAN)

THE MAN WHO VIEWS THE WORLD AT
50 THE SAME AS HE DID AT 20 HAS
WASTED 30 YEARS OF HIS LIFE.
(MUHAMMAD ALI)

IT'S NEVER TOO LATE TO
LEARN. BUT THEN IF YOU'VE
MADE IT THIS FAR . . .
WHY BOTHER?

(ANON)

THE SECRET OF IMMORTALITY IS
LIVING A LIFE WORTH REMEMBERING.
(ANON)

WE DO NOT STOP PLAYING BECAUSE
WE GROW OLD, WE GROW OLD
BECAUSE WE STOP PLAYING!
(BENJAMIN FRANKLIN)

YOUTH WASTES AWAY, BUT
IMMATURITY OFTEN
LASTS A LIFETIME.
(ANON)

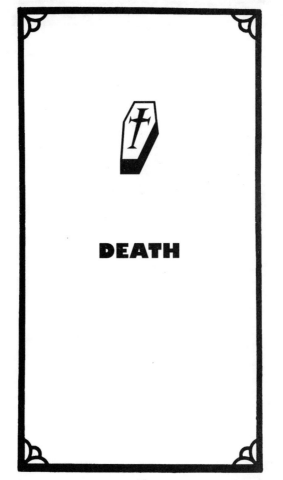

DEATH

DEATH IS
HEREDITARY.
(ANON)

DEATH ALWAYS
COMES TOO EARLY
OR TOO LATE.
(ENGLISH)

DEATH IS JUST
NATURE TELLING YOU
TO SLOW DOWN.
(ANON)

IF YOU WANT TO DIE YOUNG, MAKE
YOUR DOCTOR YOUR HEIR.
(ROMANIAN)

IT IS BETTER TO DIE LIVING
THAN TO LIVE DYING.
(ANON)

WISE MEN

A BAD EXCUSE IS BETTER THAN NONE.

(SPANISH)

A BELIEVABLE LIE IS BETTER
THAN A STUPID FACT.

(ITALIAN)

A CLOSED MOUTH CATCHES NO FLIES.

(ITALIAN)

AFTER ALL IS SAID AND DONE, MORE IS
SAID THAN DONE.

(ANON)

A CLOSED MOUTH

GATHERS NO FOOT.

(CHINESE)

ANGER IS THE OUTCOME
OF THE TONGUE WORKING
FASTER THAN THE BRAIN.

(ANON)

BEFORE YOU CRITICIZE SOMEONE,
WALK A MILE IN THEIR SHOES.
(THEN WHEN YOU DO CRITICIZE THEM,
YOU'RE A MILE AWAY AND YOU
HAVE THEIR SHOES.)

(ANON)

GOOD ADVICE IS OFTEN ANNOYING,
BAD ADVICE NEVER.

(FRENCH)

HE WHO GOSSIPS TO YOU WILL
GOSSIP ABOUT YOU.

(TURKISH)

IT IS BETTER TO CONCEAL
ONE'S KNOWLEDGE THAN TO
REVEAL ONE'S IGNORANCE.
(SPANISH)

THE DIFFERENCE BETWEEN
GENIUS AND STUPIDITY IS THAT
GENIUS HAS ITS LIMITS.
(ANON)

WHO KNOWS MOST SPEAKS LEAST.
(SPANISH)

WISDOM SHOULD NOT BE LIKE MONEY,
TIED UP AND HIDDEN.
(GHANA)

WHEN YOU OPEN A DOOR,
DON'T FORGET TO CLOSE IT.
TREAT YOUR MOUTH
ACCORDINGLY.

(JEWISH)

THE TONGUE WEIGHS
RELATIVELY NOTHING,
BUT SO FEW PEOPLE
CAN HOLD IT.

(ANON)

YOU HAVE TWO EARS
AND ONE MOUTH.
IT IS BEST TO USE
THEM IN THAT
PROPORTION.

(ANON)

FOOLS

d

ARtificial intelligence
is no match for
natural stupidity.

(ANON)

CRAFTY ADVICE IS OFTEN
GOT FROM A FOOL.
(IRISH)

EACH FOOL IS DIFFERENT.
(GERMAN)

EVERY ASS LOVES TO
HEAR HIMSELF BRAY.
(ANON)

EVERYBODY IS
IGNORANT, ONLY ON
DIFFERENT SUBJECTS.
(WILL ROGERS)

HE WHO LAUGHS
LAST LAUGHS LONGEST.
AND HAS PROBABLY
ONLY JUST GOT THE JOKE.

(ANON)

IF THERE WERE NO
FOOLS, THERE WOULD
BE NO WISE MEN.
(GERMAN)

YOUR OWN
STUPID ACTIONS
SHOULD NOT BE
CONFUSED WITH FATE.
(ANON)

NEVER
UNDERESTIMATE
THE POWER OF
STUPID PEOPLE
IN BIG GROUPS.

(ANON)

BRAVERY
&
COWARDICE

A COWARD WILL ALWAYS
THINK WITH HIS LEGS.
(ANON)

AN OLD RAT IS A BRAVE RAT.
(FRENCH)

IT IS EASY TO BE BRAVE
FROM A DISTANCE.
(NATIVE AMERICAN)

IT'S NOT THE SIZE OF THE DOG IN THE
FIGHT THAT MATTERS, IT'S THE SIZE OF
THE FIGHT IN THE DOG!
(ANON)

IT'S ALL
IN THE MIND

A CLOSED MIND
IS LIKE A CLOSED BOOK:
JUST A BLOCK OF WOOD.
(CHINESE)

GREAT SPIRITS
HAVE ALWAYS
ENCOUNTERED
VIOLENT OPPOSITION
FROM MEDIOCRE
MINDS.
(ALBERT EINSTEIN)

GReat MiNDS
DiSCUSS iDeas.

AVeRaGe MiNDS
DiSCUSS eVeNtS.

SMaLL MiNDS
DiSCUSS PeOPLe.
(ANON)

MINDS ARE LIKE
PARACHUTES: THEY ONLY
WORK WHEN OPEN.
(ANON)

TOMORROW

MANANA IS OFTEN THE
BUSIEST DAY OF THE WEEK.

(SPANISH)

NEVER PUT OFF TILL
TOMORROW WHAT MAY BE DONE
TODAY. DON'T YOU KNOW THAT
TOMORROW NEVER COMES?

(ANON)

'ONE OF THESE DAYS' MEANS
'NONE OF THESE DAYS'.

(ENGLISH)

PROCRASTINATION IS THE
THIEF OF TIME.

(ANON)

DON'T PUT OFF TILL
TOMORROW WHAT COULD
BE DONE TODAY.
WHY NOT GIVE YOURSELF
ANOTHER WEEK?

(ANON)

1

THE BEST THING ABOUT
THE FUTURE IS THAT
IT COMES ONLY
ONE DAY AT A TIME.
(ABRAHAM LINCOLN)

PATIENCE

ALL THINGS COME TO THOSE
WHO WAIT . . . BUT THE BEST THINGS
WILL BE TAKEN BY THOSE WHO
GET THERE FIRST.
(ANON)

THINGS MAY COME TO THOSE WHO
WAIT, BUT ONLY THE THINGS LEFT BY
THOSE WHO HUSTLE.
(ABRAHAM LINCOLN)

PESSIMISM

A PESSIMIST IS NEVER DISAPPOINTED.

(ANON)

HE THAT LIVES ON HOPE
WILL DIE FASTING.

(NORTH AMERICAN)

THE NAIL THAT STICKS UP IS SURE TO
BE HAMMERED DOWN.

(JAPANESE)

THE PESSIMIST SEES
DIFFICULTY IN EVERY
OPPORTUNITY. THE OPTIMIST
SEES OPPORTUNITY IN
EVERY DIFFICULTY.

(WINSTON CHURCHILL)

THERE'S NO POINT
IN TAKING LIFE SERIOUSLY;
NO-ONE GETS OUT ALIVE.

(ANON)

THE ROAD TO SUCCESS IS ALWAYS
UNDER CONSTRUCTION.

(ARNOLD PALMER)

THERE IS NO SENSE
IN BEING PESSIMISTIC.
IT WOULDN'T WORK ANYWAY.

(ANON)

YOU CANNOT UNSCRAMBLE EGGS.

(NORTH AMERICAN)

YOU'LL NEVER KNOW THE WORTH OF
THE WATER TILL THE WELL GOES DRY.

(SCOTTISH)

TRUTH
&
LIES

A LIE TRAVELS ROUND THE
WORLD WHILE TRUTH IS STILL
PUTTING ON HER BOOTS.
(FRENCH)

A LITTLE TRUTH WILL HELP
THE LIE GO DOWN.
(ITALIAN)

CRAFTINESS MUST HAVE
CLOTHES BUT TRUTH LIKES
TO GO NAKED.
(ENGLISH)

HISTORY IS A CATALOGUE
OF LIES COMPILED
BY THOSE IN CHARGE.

(ANON)

IF YOU BELIEVE EVERYTHING YOU
READ, BETTER NOT READ.
(JAPANESE)

LIES NEVER SETTLE THE PAYMENT.
(CROATIAN)

ONCE IN A WHILE YOU WILL STUMBLE
UPON THE TRUTH BUT MOST OF US
MANAGE TO PICK OURSELVES UP
AND HURRY ALONG AS IF NOTHING
HAD HAPPENED.
(WINSTON CHURCHILL)

ONE LIE RUINS A THOUSAND TRUTHS.
(SOUTH AFRICA)

A RUMOUR GOES
IN ONE EAR AND
OUT MANY MOUTHS.
(CHINESE)

SPEAK THE TRUTH,
BUT THEN LEAVE IMMEDIATELY.
(SLOVENIA)

'THEY SAY SO,' IS HALF A LIE.
(ITALIAN)

TRUTH AND OIL WILL ALWAYS MAKE
THEIR WAY TO THE SURFACE.
(SPANISH)

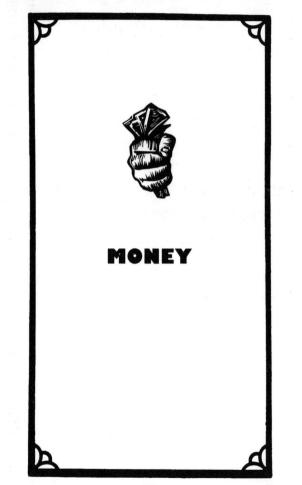

MONEY

A PIG BOUGHT
ON CREDIT
IS FOREVER
GRUNTING.
(SPANISH)

DON'T OFFER ME
ADVICE:
GIVE ME MONEY.
(SPANISH)

IF YOU THINK NO-ONE CARES
WHETHER YOU'RE DEAD OR ALIVE,
TRY MISSING A COUPLE OF
MORTGAGE PAYMENTS.

(ANON)

IF RICH PEOPLE COULD HIRE
OTHER PEOPLE TO DIE FOR THEM,
POOR PEOPLE WOULD MAKE A
WONDERFUL LIVING.

(YIDDISH)

IF YOU LEND SOMEONE
£10 AND NEVER SEE THEM
AGAIN, IT WAS PROBABLY
WORTH IT.

(ANON)

LEND YOUR MONEY AND
LOSE YOUR FRIEND.
(ENGLISH)

MONEY AND THE DEVIL DO NOT REST.
(SERBIAN)

RATHER FAIL
WITH HONOUR THAN
SUCCEED BY FRAUD.
(SOPHOCLES)

TO BE RICH IS NOT
EVERYTHING, BUT IT
CERTAINLY HELPS.
(YIDDISH)

THE QUICKEST WAY
TO DOUBLE YOUR MONEY
IS TO FOLD IT IN HALF
AND PUT IT BACK IN
YOUR POCKET.

(ANON)

££££££££££

YOUNG GAMBLERS,
OLD BEGGARS.

(GERMAN)

HAPPINESS

HAPPINESS IS ALL ABOUT
LIKING WHAT YOU DO AND
DOING WHAT YOU LIKE.

(ANON)

HAPPINESS IS NOT HAVING WHAT YOU
WANT, BUT WANTING WHAT YOU HAVE.

(ANON)

TAKE RISKS: IF YOU WIN, YOU
WILL BE HAPPY; IF YOU DON'T
YOU WILL BE WISE.

(ANON)

THE LESS YOU UNDERSTAND, THE
HAPPIER YOU WILL BE.

(ANON)

YOU CAN TURN DOLLARS INTO CENTS,
OR SENSE INTO DOLLARS, BUT NOT
DOLLARS INTO SENSE.

(AMERICAN)

117

FRIENDS
&
FOES

BETTER A FRIENDLY REFUSAL THAN
AN UNWILLING ACCEPTANCE.

(GERMAN)

BOTH YOUR FRIEND AND YOUR ENEMY
THINK YOU WILL NEVER DIE.

(IRISH)

FLATTERY MAKES FRIENDS;
TRUTH ENEMIES.

(SPANISH)

FEED YOUR HORSE AS YOU WOULD A
FRIEND BUT MOUNT HIM AS AN ENEMY.

(CROATIAN)

FRIENDS ARE LIKE FIDDLE
STRINGS; THEY MUST NOT BE
SCREWED TOO TIGHT.

(ENGLISH)

GOOD FENCES MAKE
GOOD NEIGHBOURS
(THEY KEEP THE SODS OUT!)
(ANON)

A GUILTY CONSCIENCE
IS A LIVELY ENEMY.
(INDIAN)

LIFE WITH NO FRIENDS IS LIKE
DEATH WITH NO WITNESSES.
(SPANISH)

LOVE YOUR NEIGHBOURS, BUT DON'T
PULL DOWN THE FENCE.
(CHINESE)

LOVE YOUR ENEMIES;
IT'S GUARANTEED TO
PISS THEM OFF!

(ANON)

WHEN YOUR ENEMY FALLS,
DON'T REJOICE. BUT DON'T
PICK HIM UP EITHER.

(YIDDISH)

yes, forgive your
enemies whenever
you can, but always
remember their names.

(ANON)

WOMEN

A BAD LABOUR, AND
A DAUGHTER AFTER ALL.

(SPANISH)

A BLIND MAN'S WIFE
NEEDS NO PAINT.

(SPANISH)

A HOUSE WITHOUT A WOMAN IS THE
DEVIL'S OWN LODGING.

(INDIAN)

AS THE BEST WINE MAKES THE
SHARPEST VINEGAR, SO CAN THE
TRUEST LOVER TURN INTO THE
WORST ENEMY.

(ANON)

A BEAUTIFUL WOMAN
BELONGS TO EVERYONE
BUT AN UGLY WOMAN
IS ALL YOURS.

(INDIAN)

CHOOSE NEITHER A WOMAN NOR
LINEN BY CANDLELIGHT.
(ITALIAN)

FORTUNE IS LIKE A WOMAN:
IF YOU NEGLECT HER TODAY, DO NOT
EXPECT TO REGAIN HER TOMORROW.
(FRENCH)

THERE ARE TWO THEORIES
ABOUT ARGUING WITH WOMEN.
NEITHER WORKS.
(ANON)

AGE IS THE ONLY TOPIC WOMEN
WILL KEEP QUIET ABOUT.
(GERMAN)

MEN

A MAN IS A PERSON WHO TAKES OUT
THE RUBBISH, THEN MAKES OUT HE
HAS JUST CLEANED THE HOUSE.

(ANON)

BEHIND EVERY SUCCESSFUL
MAN THERE'S A GREAT . . .
NAG, NAG, NAG.

(ANON)

MARRIAGE

A DEAF HUSBAND AND A BLIND WIFE
ARE THE PERFECT HAPPY COUPLE.

(ANON)

A JEALOUS LOVER WILL BECOME AN
INDIFFERENT SPOUSE.

(MEXICAN)

A POOR BEAUTY FINDS MORE LOVERS
THAN HUSBANDS.

(ENGLISH)

A GOOD HUSBAND IS
HEALTHY AND ABSENT.

(JAPANESE)

A wife is frightened of her first husband. A husband is frightened of his second wife.

(Serbian)

A wife's advice is not worth much, but woe to the husband who refuses to take it.

(Welsh)

He who marries for money will earn it.

(American)

If you want to be criticized, get married.

(Irish)

MARRIAGE IS LIKE A GROUND NUT,
YOU MUST CRACK IT TO
SEE WHAT'S INSIDE.
(GHANA)

NEVER MAKE A
PRETTY WOMAN
YOUR WIFE.
(JAMAICAN)

GRIEF FOR A HUSBAND
IS LIKE A PAIN IN THE ELBOW
– SHARP AND SHORT.
(ENGLISH)

THE FIRST MARRIAGE
IS A DISH OF HONEY,
THE SECOND A GLASS OF WINE,
THE THIRD A CUP OF POISON.
(SERBIAN)

NEVER MARRY FOR
MONEY; YOU WILL
BORROW IT CHEAPER.
(SCOTTISH)

GOD
& THE
DEVIL

BE NEITHER INTIMATE
NOR DISTANT WITH
THE CLERGY.
(IRISH)

BETTER THE DEVIL
YOU KNOW THAN
THE DEVIL YOU DON'T.
(ENGLISH)

GOD GIVES THE NUTS,
BUT HE DOESN'T
CRACK THEM.
(GERMAN)

GOD IS BIGGER
THAN YOUR
PROBLEMS.
(MEXICAN)

GOD SUPPLIES
THE MILK
BUT NOT THE JUG.
(GERMAN)

HE WHO SUPS WITH
THE DEVIL HAS NEED
OF A LONG SPOON.

(ENGLISH)

IF GOD DIDN'T
FORGIVE SINNERS,
HEAVEN WOULD
BE EMPTY.
(GERMAN)

IF GOD LIVED ON
EARTH, PEOPLE WOULD
BREAK HIS WINDOWS.
(JEWISH)

IF THE PATIENT DIES,
THE DOCTOR HAS KILLED HIM;
IF HE GETS WELL, THE
SAINTS HAVE SAVED HIM.
(ITALIAN)

THE DEVIL'S
BOOTS
DON'T CREAK.
(SCOTTISH)

THE DEVIL
NEVER GRANTS
LONG LEASES.

(IRISH)

we are all equal in
the eyes of god and
bus drivers.

(GERMAN)

P.C.
PROVERBS

A JOURNEY OF a
THOUSAND SITES BEGINS
WITH JUST ONE CLICK.

DON'T BYTE OFF
MORE THAN YOU
CAN VIEW.

THE EMAIL OF
THE SPECIES IS FAR
DEADLIER THAN
THE MAIL.

FAX IS STRANGER
THAN FICTION.

IN GATES WE TRUST.

YOU CAN'T TEACH A
NEW MOUSE
OLD CLICKS.

THE MESSAGE IS
IN THE MODEM.

THE GEEK
SHALL INHERIT
THE EARTH.

TOO MANY
CLICKS SPOIL
THE MESSAGE.

USERS AND THEIR
LEISURE TIME
ARE SOON PARTED.

VIRTUAL REALITY IS
ITS OWN REWARD.

WHAT BOOTS UP
MUST COME DOWN.

WINDOWS WILL
NEVER CEASE.

www.crombiejardine.com